The Adventures of Alixa Doom

and other
love poems
by

Philip Dacey

copyright 2003 by Philip Dacey
Published by Snark Publishing
www.snarkpub.com
Snark Chapbooks Series #22

cover art by Susan Montag
Set in Electra LT by PF Allen
To order: send $5 to

PF Allen
Snark Publishing
637 W Hwy 50 #119
O'Fallon IL 62269

Contents

Jackpot Junction 1

Sleeping With the CIA 3

The Adventures of Alixa Doom 4

Leg 5

Going Steady at 62 6

Appoggiaturas 7

Canoeing in the Bedroom 8

Cover to Cover 10

On the Road 11

Apart 13

Reunions 14

Love in Public 16

For the Lares and Penates 18

Massaging Her Feet 20

From the Front 21

The Apology 23

Guest of Honor 24

for Alixa,
my eponymous Muse —
"Who was that masked woman?"

ACKNOWLEDGEMENTS

Poems herein have appeared in print as follows:

Atlanta Review: "From the Front"
Aura Literary Arts Review: "Sleeping With the CIA"
Cumberland Poetry Review: "The Apology," "Guest of Honor"
Cumball Poetry: "Leg"
Hampden-Sydney Poetry Review: "The Music of"
Margie: "Driving at Dawn"
One Trick Pony: "Appoggiaturas," "Self-Portrait as Lover"
Poet Lore: "Canoeing in the Bedroom"
Steam Ticket: "Apart," "Codes."
Poetry International: "Cover to Cover"

"Leg" was reprinted in the anthology *Touched by Eros* (Live Poets Society, 2002).

"From the Front" won an International Merit Award in *Atlanta Review's* 2003 International Poetry Competition.

"Guest of Honor" was read by Garrison Keillor as part of his Writer's Almanac, Minnesota Public Radio (Jan. 31, 2003).

JACKPOT JUNCTION

It began at a casino,
as if to make a point.
Almost a first date, almost blind.
Fortuna as ruling goddess.
Later, his heart all shuffled again
and about to be dealt out on his sleeve,
he felt like history;
which is to say,
hope against the odds.

So many other games in town—
real estate, for instance,
or stamp collecting—yet here he was
playing this one again.
Maybe it was the shape of the table
where someone who held all the cards sat,
how the shape kept changing,
or the mysterious hieroglyphics
painted on the felt.
He'd searched his pockets and found,
to his surprise, another coin—
gold, the dead man embossed on it
looking uncannily like him.

So they walked around among
the slots—he and this woman
who looked like the jackpot—
through the racket of color, the long rows of faces
as grim as those of criminals awaiting sentencing.

Anyone near the couple
might have seen reflected in their eyes
enough flashing and spinning
to make them look like cartoon characters
who'd just been hit on the head,
addled but innocent creatures,
at home in the Sunday funnies.
What he couldn't have explained, however, if asked,
was how any innocence at all persisted
this late, this near closing time,
though he might have figured
there was always the chance,
and it was worth betting on.

SLEEPING WITH THE CIA

When his girlfriend told him
she'd worked for the CIA,
he wanted to search her entire body
for microphones. Just as he'd
always suspected: love

had a cover, a false name,
and could be spirited out of town
when the heat was on.
McLean, Virginia, was home
to the complete dossier

on Cupid, definitely
a suspicious character
whose circle needed
to be infiltrated.
Istanbul, the Baltic Sea,

these were part of her job,
why she'd been told as she left,
"Remember, you never worked for us."
Thirty years she kept the secret.
Then that night, and their pillow talk

turned radioactive.
He was Peace Corps, she CIA,
young feds, and naive. They'd gone
to different schools together.
He kissed every microphone.

THE ADVENTURES OF ALIXA DOOM

When I told my friends I was dating
Alixa Doom, ex-CIA agent,
they didn't believe me.
They wanted to know what comic book
I'd lifted that character from

and said they might want to read it
themselves. And when I insisted
she was real, my literary friends said,
"Sure, real like Marianne Moore's
real toads in imaginary gardens."

So I gave up. I agreed with them
she was a cartoon character
but reminded them I was one, too,
just like each of them, the balloons
full of hot-air words always floating

above our heads, our dimensions three
only on our best days, and our colors
so bright as obviously to have been
painted in by a talented child
playing God. "Kapow!" I said, and all

my friends showed up in the same
framed panel, bug-eyed to witness
my heroine, with the merest touch
of her knowing hand, get the goods on
this world in saddle stitch.

LEG

Driving at night, I reached across for the knee
your skirt failed to cover and soon had your
long left leg and thigh bared in the dark car,
my hand like that of one blind who could see
by touching, fondling. You leaned back with a sigh.
South Dakota. The Great Plains. Summer stars.
A white glow, your leg lit up the interior
and by its slim self tamed the wandering sky:
I swear all that vast space surrounding us
pressed in close, closer, to the curving glass,
the prodigal void finally come home.
My left hand steered straight, my right strayed, overcome
by a silkiness some fire must have learned.
The hand that writes this, held there, burned and burned.

GOING STEADY AT 62

What would their friends,
their grown children,
say? And how interpret
a high school ring that depicted
St. Louis on a horse and thorns

twisted into a crown?
Something about power, a journey,
pain transformed by time into
triumph? "Serious joke,"
was how the two planned to break

the news, though his thumb,
which had always liked
touching the silver and gold,
now returned empty-handed
from its little jaunt across the palm,

the absence measured over
and over. He couldn't forget
he'd given himself away,
that somewhere else he was happily
wrapped around a finger, another thumb

reaching out to explore his cool,
embossed skin. And when she moved
her hand through the air, he was
a man in motion, carried away;
he had the sensation of flying.

COVER TO COVER

She loves the times they read in bed together,
even the interruptions, a quote, a touch. The sound
of pages in motion, one passage after another.
She fiction, he history. Or poems, a bond.

Passion as prologue or epilogue, usually,
but this more intimate, the book a kind
of lover, who penetrates in such a way
that she opens all the more to him at her side.

Two lamps, and country night pressed close against
the skylight, a reader peering over a shoulder,
and the arrogantly illiterate stars for once
envious, aware of the word but left out in the cold.

His left foot reads her right. The moment's ample,
their bookmarks sacred, fixtures in the temple.

the condition their prow constantly pierced
and entered and slipped beyond
as they thought to hold hands,
as if hands so joined were rudders,

or a memory of rudders, unless memory
itself was a rudder, useless of course
in any canoe given over to the current,
which loved paddles, memories, rudders,

whatever rode it, but especially
bedrooms, how they could, despite their bulk,
be lifted and carried easily, buoyant
in the afternoon sun through their windows.

CANOEING IN THE BEDROOM

At first merely a languorous mood,
afternoon sun through the bedroom window,
dispelling the winter,
weighting their eyelids,

until the words "passive" and "vulnerable"
rose between them, like a wave, lips
hovering near lips, the silence afterwards
a downward pull less gravity than current,

the occasion for drift and the will
to surrender the will, for the next wordwave,
"like two in a canoe," as a hand outside the bed
thrilled to trail in water, releasing purls,

and the couple lay flat on their backs
in the hull, only the finite sky of the infinite ceiling
visible overhead, the paddles lost among
the bedcovers, never to be found again

in the descent, downriver, to sleep, and dream,
or to a wakefulness more dream than anything
in sleep, so that the source of a sound
like that of rapids, a roar in the ear, blood

forcing its way, a falls,
could not be located for sure
in either past or future, behind or in front,
all knowledge reduced now to a mist above a river,

APPOGGIATURAS

When the rose died, I saved the petals and spread
them all across the sheet where soon she'd lie.
That night, we lived our love on a field of red
gestures, a luxury of grace notes, but I

didn't anticipate how far the story
would go, that when she sat up afterwards
her back and side would shock me with its glory
of stuck petals, small mouths, like beautiful wounds,

or that all of the next morning we'd strew
from both of our bodies throughout the house
proof that the mutual wild dream was true
and, even better, that we ourselves were flowers.

No wonder I've come here on my knees to sing
of the solemn mysteries of gardening.

ON THE ROAD

1. Travelling Towards His Lover

There are no mountains between us,
though there seem to be.
The horizon mocks and mocks.
This automobile must have a love
in the opposite direction.

The clouds translate your name
into clouds. All farms
are harvesting tributes to your hair.
Speed may kill, but slowness wounds.
As sideroads tempt me in vain,

a dead deer reminds me
of the seriousness of your kisses.
The road's curve traces your hip.
Now a schoolbus the color
of my happy anticipation

passes a silo that mimics
a finger pointing the way.
The suspension system dreams
of your smooth skin. A river valley
promises décolletage; I let

a country church look to the afterlife.
Broken center lines, whole ones,
time together, time apart.
A stab of jealousy:
the dashboard will reach you first.

2. Driving at Dawn

Someone somewhere
is getting an idea.
My lights
make a tunnel in darkness.
Grandfather, who followed the veins

of coal,
sing me a song.
One star
is a third headlamp.
I've left my love

in her bed;
though beautiful,
the road is sad.
A great creature crawls
from its lair and stretches

across the far horizon.
Even stones
are in motion, rest
an illusion.
None of the other drivers

is a stranger.
From watertower to watertower
we go.
The idea's bigger now,
with color in its cheeks.

APART

Days together, then an empty bed,
department of missing person.
Playing field on which
to play nothing.
Reverse suffocation:

the mouth dangerously free
to press itself against air.
The flung covers form
the Chinese character
for solitary.

I know the answer to the riddle:
When is a whole bed
a half a bed?
In the dark, I pretend
you are a negative

of yourself, glowing black,
while the pillows do bad imitations
of your hips, breasts.
I lie, arms crossed,
like one after his death.

The moon through the skylight
searches for you, too.
Now the bed is a raft,
the vast sea your absence,
and I hoist the sail of this poem.

REUNIONS

1. The Music of

After a long separation,
celebrating our reunion
with my head between her legs,
I heard music. Choral. Strings maybe.

Palestrina? A sacred sound. I only
half listened to what I assumed
was the radio, which somehow
had gotten turned on.

Afterwards, a surprising silence.
What happened to the music? She'd
heard nothing, saying my love
must have tapped into the realm

of spirit, and quoted Valery: "There is
another world, and it is in this one."
No Palestrina. I should have
listened more carefully. Brought back

a musical phrase like a voiceprint.
I'd cheer the composer, if I could locate
him, her, it. In the meantime,
I like to imagine the obscure one's

complete oeuvre
and the scholars and connoisseurs
who've devoted their lives
to every note, half note, rest.

2. Self-Portrait as Lover

A reunion at their favorite restaurant,
he so happy to see her that, afterwards,
as they drive in separate cars to her place,
he hates the distance between them.

The food excellent, but no matter,
the taste of the road is terrible.
Both the heavy traffic and the night
keep hiding her somewhere in front of him—

he chews on his faith. Such mockery
of taillights, little medieval devils!
And didn't he once think his mother
abandoned him in a store? Now he knows:

a five-year-old is driving this car.
But as he spots her on the exit ramp,
he feels something deep in his brain
and helplessly subject to a force

like gravity steer the car her way;
no longer even a child, he could be part
of a great vee of geese, out of this world,
surveying a chain of frozen lakes.

Pulling into her driveway, he waves
and smiles at the eyes in her rearview mirror,
a creature successfully impersonating
a grown-up man in control of his life.

LOVE IN PUBLIC

1. Dramaturgy

It was my idea to stage
a classic romantic scene
roadside for the benefit
of black leather, a caravan

of motorcycles I could see
would soon pass us as we stood
on the wetlands bridge listening
to frogs celebrate the mud.

I said, "Kiss me," and bent you
back and sideways, Broadway-style,
my arms cradling you, who leaned
like an actress into the role

just as the gang of Angels
roared by all wheels and steel
and helmetless turning of
heads, their critics' approval

signalled by no commotion
of hands but, better, non-
stop honking to outdo any
opening night standing ovation,

for we were seasoned thespians
who knew just how to move
to triumph in the play
(long-running!) called spring and love.

2. Codes

She likes referring in public
to his private part,
which she likes, and which
they named, after a character
in early Fellini, Zampano,

an itinerant strongman
specializing in breaking chains
across his chest. Therefore it's
Zampano this and Zampano that
in restaurants, in lines at the movies.

Because it pleases her to talk
so openly in secret
of what gives her pleasure, or who,
she has come to understand
the satisfaction of codes,

the sending of messages
under the nose of the oppressor,
whose agents are everywhere,
how the acolytes of Eros,
that dangerous subversive,

freely do the work of their god
by playing the game
of a double life,
like a heart on a sleeve
that passes for a food stain.

FOR THE LARES AND PENATES

1. Skylight Song

Stars through the skylight,
stars in your hair,
love unlimited,
bordered by a square.

With the outside in
and the inside out,
space is our home,
deep black our sheets.

What falls flaringly
enters your dream.
I'll catch you again
when the morning comes.

2. Love Seat Song

No room for three.
Too much room for one.
Come sit with me
and be my love.

Shoulder to shoulder,
down the road.
This love seat's moving
at its own good speed.

More than furniture,
upholstered future.
The whole house shifts
for this new center.

Why wait, why hesitate?
Indoors, outdoors,
day and night,
let's live in the love seat.

MASSAGING HER FEET

This little piggy
enters my dreams.
The fit of heel in palm—
continents a single landmass
before the cataclysm.

A finger slides between
two toes; snake in the grass.
Where does the cream go?
I want to follow it.
The sisters Left

and Right have carried you
to me. With the instep
as yin and the ball
of the sole as yang, I trace
the shape of the universe.

Two mute serving girls,
years in the cellar,
restored by the hand
to their royal place and wearing
peppermint crowns.

A spreading flush: dawn
inside the foot. Suddenly
I'm Mary Magdalene,
kneeling, long hair
brushing the robe of God.

FROM THE FRONT

"War is the ultimate story,"
the frontline correspondent
says on the radio.

I'm having my breakfast,
pouring the un-ultimate milk
over my un-ultimate cornflakes.

No one's shooting at me here.
I'm only breathing, sprinkling sugar
like a light snow.

I love the woman across from me,
the way she sips her coffee,
the cup in both hands,

though the story we're in,
I've been told,
lacks something.

I reach across the table
and touch her arm, as if she were
one of the wounded, and I

a chaplain, or nurse. She smiles
a smile from the story of peace,
of two people learning

not to go to war
against each other,
the story whose chapter

of blank pages says so much
about the art of story-telling,
ultimately.

THE APOLOGY

> "Sex on beach: couple must
> apologize in print as sentence."
> CNN Headline News, June 28, 2002

The sand's give invited us, and we didn't see
the children. The waves' susurrus lulled
us into a false sense of security.
We saw boats on the horizon, their hulls

gleaming smooth and hard in the sun, like buff
bodies at our health club. Once a beach ball
rolled by but its colors made us think of
the earthly garden itself in space, how all

its pleasures were speeding away, and the voices we heard,
vertiginous, were like inner ones urging us on
to chase after the day, catch it and wrestle it hard
down against the shore. Make it ours. Just then

the sandpiper's dash past our feet said, "Hurry, hurry."
The deed's done now, washed out with the tide. We're sorry.

GUEST OF HONOR

Every day, I drive by the grave
of my fiancee's father.
She lost him when she was one.
He's our intimate stranger,

our guardian angel,
floating a la Chagall
just above our heads.
I go to him for love lessons.

He touches my hand
with that tenderness
the dead have for the living.
When I touch her hand so,

she knows where I've been.
At the wedding,
he'll give her away to me.
And the glass he'll raise to toast us

will be a chalice brimful of sun,
his words heard all the more clearly
for their absence, as stone
is cut away to form dates.